DIVISION OF SPOILS

DIVISION OF SPOILS
SELECTED POEMS
J. D. McClatchy

2003

Published by Arc Publications
Nanholme Mill, Shaw Wood Road
Todmorden, Lancs OL14 6DA, UK

© J. D. McClatchy 2003

Design by Tony Ward
Cover design by Chip Kidd
Print by Antony Rowe Ltd.,
Eastbourne, East Sussex

ISBN 1 900072 65 3

Cover photograph of sculpture by
Antonio Canova at the Canova Museum,
Possagno, Veneto, Italy by Richard Bryant.
By permission of Arcaid.

This edition is published by arrangement
with Alfred A. Knopf, a division of
Random House, Inc.

The Publishers acknowledge financial
assistance from Yorkshire Arts Board

**Arc Publications International Poets
Series Editor: John Kinsella**

CONTENTS

The Ledger / 7

from *The Rest of The Way* (1990)

Medea in Tokyo / 11
The Shield of Herakles / 12
Zion / 15
The Rented House / 17
Heads / 19
Fog Tropes / 21
The Window / 27
Kilim / 28

from *Ten Commandments* (1998)

My Early Hearts / 39
My Mammogram / 42
Found Parable / 45
My Sideshow / 47
Under Hydra / 49
Proust in Bed / 51
Tea with the Local Saint / 54
Chott / 57
What They Left Behind / 59
After Ovid / 60
The Dialogue of Desire and Guilt / 62
Flies / 64
Honest Iago / 65
Auden's OED / 66
Three Dreams About Elizabeth Bishop / 71
Late Night Ode / 74

New Poems

Tattoos / 77
Glanum / 87

About the Author / 91

for Chip Kidd

THE LEDGER

Love is injustice, said Camus.
We want to be loved. What's still more true?
Each wants most to be preferred,
And listens for those redeeming words
Better than X, more than Y –
Enough to quiet the child's cry,
The bridegroom's nerves, the patient's
Reluctant belief in providence.
Break what you can, hurt whom you will,
Humiliate the others until
Someone takes a long, hard look.
Oh Love, put down your balance book.

from
The Rest of the Way
(1990)

MEDEA IN TOKYO

Already in place, her tears are chainlink gold,
Her grief a silken streamer of "blood" that friends
Draw slowly from her mouth while she is told
A rival has worked her magic. Who's the witch?
The unseen girl will have her hour, then ends
Up on fire. And the star's in fact an old
Man, with clay breasts and trailing robe
Forty pounds of mirror flints enrich,
Who never says a word I comprehend.

What happens when the language is a mask,
And the words we use to hush this up have failed?
The chorus – beekeepers with samisen – ask
That question (I think) over and over again.
Is tragedy finally wrenched from fairy tale
When we ought to understand but can't pretend?

She doesn't hear a thing. Her dragon cart –
The bucket of a sleek hydraulic lift –
Sways above us all. By now the part
Has worn out her revenge. We're made to feel
Even she is beyond the spell of speech, the gift
Of fate she gave the others. But a moral starts
To echo. The children's screams. And to each wheel
A body's tied with ribbons, pale and stiff.
The words had made no sense, but the sword was real.

THE SHIELD OF HERAKLES

The ocean circles its outer rim,
With dented silver swan-shaped studs
To hold taut the backing, deerskin
Lashed to a frame of olive wood.

Next, as if on shore, a round
Of horsemen, loosening their reins,
Gaining on a prize forever unwon.
The face of each is worked in pain.

(Who once coughed up the Milky Way
And later, maddened, killed his sons
Has guiltily now to undertake
Labours to please a weaker man.)

And then a city with seven gates
Of gold where men are bringing home
A bride in her high-wheeled chariot.
Shrill bridal pipes and their echo

Mingle with the swollen torches,
Women, one foot lifted to the lyre,
And a pack of young men watching
Or laughing in the dance, tired,

Others mounted, galloping past
A field the ploughman's just turned up.
Sharpened hooks have reaped the last
Bending stalks that children prop

In sheaves. Beside them now a row
Of vines, with ivory tendrils curled
On grapes soon trod upon to draw
Their sweetness for the frightened girl.

(My journal of dreams this month: "One
By one the twelve new monsters yield."
The doctor says the threat's begun
To counterattack. Is strength a shield?)

Deeper within stand ranks of men
In warring harness, to hold or sack
The town, while corpses, enemy by friend,
Lie near widows tearing their cheeks –

They could have been alive. The Fates,
Shrouded in black enamel, loom
Behind, clawing a soldier to taste
The blood that drips from an open wound.

And closer still four faces stare –
Panic, Slaughter, Chaos, Dread –
Each knotted to the next one's hair
By serpents, like the Gorgon's head.

And here are souls now swept beneath
The world, all made of palest glass,
Their skin and bones long since bequeathed
To earth, where the wandering stars pass.

(The archers squint at a gleaming phalanx,
As if from nowhere moved into place.
Machine-made Armageddons – tanks
Or missile shields in outer space –

Threaten always to turn against
The false-hearted power they excite.
What draws attack is self-defence,
A target for the arrow's flight.)

And at its very centre, a wonder
Held up to see, the figure of Fear
Was hammered fast by fire and thunder.
But only half her face appears.

The other half is turned away,
A quivering lip, one widened eye,
Turned back as if to warn in vain
The armoured giant, come to rely

On what protects to terrify,
That while at night his dreams explain
The city and field, the dance, the bride,
A crow is picking at one of the slain.

ZION

     Twin cloud mesas abut
the Angels Landing, as the sun
slips around the caprock one last maize-gold
     cinch that swallows tighten,
running laces of thin air back
and forth across the fractured sandstone edge

     with its beadwork a snow
melt had left of manzanita,
pinyon pine (bent double), and that paintbrush
     just barely visible
to your zoom lens from the canyon
floor, near the Virgin, where we watch and wait.

     The rust-run strikes remind
how much gravel and limey ooze,
dead weighted by layers of fossil shells
     and bones and flood plain tracks,
has hardened into shapes we can
call up our feelings by, the worn surface

     of time laid down in arcs
or crossbedded ruts the wind makes
for water to erode. Look what's happened
     even here. The river,
rain-swollen, swept shale and boulder,
its very banks – the arguments of waste

     that years accumulate –
downstream to oceans drop by drop
returned in thunderheads to their stripping
     work. But something resists.
The steepest ramparts hold themselves
apart for the time being, unmindful

       of anything but scale
and distance, light and old beliefs.
Altar, Temple, Throne – the high places named,
       like features of a life
together that endures, the sky's
empty place kept waiting behind them all,

       or like the gospel song –
when we've been there ten thousand years,
bright shining as the sun, we've no less days
       (here on the middle step
of what they call the Grand Stairway)
to sing God's praise than when we first begun.

THE RENTED HOUSE

The faintly digital click of the overhead fan
    stroking what was left of the dark
had finally given way to a rooster alarm.
    Not that we needed one.

We'd been kept awake all night by cats, cats
    in the crawlspace, in the yard,
up and down the back lane, until it seemed
    they were in your head,

their guttural chittering, then a courting sound –
    more like tyres spinning on ice –
a sort of erotic simmer that would mount
    to a wail in heat, a wailing,

one pair, and soon after another, the same,
    sex shrieking all around and under us,
who hadn't touched, or barely spoken, for days.
    When I leaned over you

to bang on the window, your back was hot on my chest.
    I banged louder, longer, less to scare
the cats away than to feel your heat, the flesh
    and an inch above the flesh,

while listening to theirs, though theirs hurt less
    because the pain thrilled, you could hear it,
the now worried tom helplessly caught in her
    until she'd had enough.

And then they set to fighting. Again and again
    I'd be getting out of bed to stamp or shout
into the dark, and they would stop for a minute
    before turning on each other

with a threatening sigh-long cough. No point, no use
    trying to silence it. And the losers,
self-pitying, moved off further under the house,
    making a curious new sound,

a wounded coo and some hen-gabble (Christ!
    I should have known that rooster was a cat).
By morning we were all exhausted, trying to start
    something or stop it,

giving in to another day, angry – but angry at what?
    There on the porch, when I opened the screen door,
a black, three-legged, pregnant cat was sitting,
    our brooding household god,

last night's own story staring back at me in the slatted
    early palmlight, all the accidents of envy and will
thrown together in one mangled, swollen creature,
    mewling, limping, her stump

dangling down beneath her belly. When I took one,
    then two hesitant steps toward her, she arched
and hobbled away. Sometimes a life comes to its senses,
    or suddenly just speeds up,

as when we first met, whole months it seemed collapsed
    to a night, an emptiness years-deep filled
and spilling over by dawn into – but first things first.
    Some milk. A shallow bowl.

By the time I'd returned with it, the cat had vanished.
    But there beside the door, earlier overlooked,
you'd already set a milkbowl down for her yourself,
    someone else's earthenware,

the glazed, coarse-grained gesture neither of us
    can make for each other. Poor, stupid cat,
where are you? All day the bowls have sat there,
    side by side, untouched.

HEADS

Jerusalem, November 1987

As if layered in a wedge of honey cake,
    The aromas of split persimmon,
        Mint, cat spray, and cardamom
    All mingle with the bitter coffee
        On this morning's scuffed brass tray
Brought into the shop by a cripple with wings.

The match for two Marlboros also now strikes
    The end to one loud bit of holy
        ("Faith" in Arabic is "*din*")
    Bargaining at the end of the street.
        Peels of old light lie scattered
Outside. Dogs barking. Market day in the souk.

Muhammad deals in goat heads. His rival's shop
    Is beef, swags of lung and counters heaped
        With livers like paving stones,
    A child-high pile of squat, outsize shins
        And marbleized, harelipped hearts –
Food the rich man eats to settle his conscience.

And there are flies next door, and a hose to wash
    Dung out of the cow guts... which reminds
        Muhammad of his brother
    Who left to become headwaiter at
        Rasputin's Piano-Bar.
Both his grandfathers, his father too, had worked

In this tiled hollow lit by one bare bulb.
    Stuck in the mirror are their postcards
        Of the Kaaba, the silk-veiled,
    Quartz-veined sky-stone, Islam's one closed eye.
        Muhammad hasn't made his
Required pilgrimage. He went west instead,

The hajj to California, but came up six
   Credits shy at Fresno State. (Shy too
      Of the girlfriend who'd wanted
   To marry "for good," not a green card.)
      So he's back in the shop now,
Next to a copper tub of boiling water.

He takes another head by the ear and dips
   It – *eight, nine, ten* – into the kettle,
      Then quickly starts to shave it
   With a bone-handled wartime Gilette.
      The black matted shag falls in
Patches to the floor and floats toward the clogged drain.

One after another, the heads are stacked up .
   Behind, like odd-lot, disassembled
      Plastic replicas of goats.
   Though their lips are hardened now, the teeth
      Of some can be seen – perfect!
But Muhammad hacks the jaws off anyway,

And the skulls with their nubbly horns and ears.
   What's left is meant for his faithful poor,
      For their daily meager stew.
   He lines up six on a shelf out front.
      (As if all turned inside out,
The heads, no longer heads exactly, strangely

Bring to mind relief maps of the "occupied
   Territories." Born on the wrong side
      Of a new border, he's made
   To carry his alien's ID,
      Its sullen headshot labelled
In the two warring tongues.) Goat heads feed them all,

The refugee, the single man, and his dog –
   Their delicacy. Cartilage knobs.
      Fat sacs. The small cache of flesh.
   The eyeballs staring out at nothing
      In all directions. The tongue
Lolling up, as if with something more to say.

FOG TROPES

A sheet of water turned over.
Sedge script. River erasure.
The smoke out of the factory
Stacks drifts to the title page –
Words too big to read, too quickly
Gone to say what they are.
The water machine is stalled
And sighs. There go last night's
Now forgotten dreams, airborne,
Homebound, on their way to work.

*

Again this morning: five-storey elm spoons
Stirring the wheylight, fur on the knobby
Melon rind left in the sink, the china egg
Under the laying hen, the quilt's missing
Patch, and now the full moon's steamed-up
Shaving mirror leaning against the blue.

*

When my daughter died, from the bottom
Of every pleasure something bitter
Rose up, a sour taste of nausea,
The certain sense of having failed
Not to save her but in the end to know
I could not keep her from passing
As through the last, faintest intake
Of breath to somewhere unsure of itself,
The dim landscape that grief supposes.
I remember how, in the hospital,
Without a word she put her glasses on
And stared ahead, just before she died.

I take mine off these days, to see
More of my solitude, its incidental
Humiliations. Nothing satisfies
Its demand that she appear in order
To leave my life over and over again.
If, from my car, I should glimpse her
In a doorway, bright against the dark
Inside, and stop and squint at the glare –
It's a rag on a barbed-wire fence.
Or I spot her in a sidewalk crowd
But almost at once she disappears
The way one day slips behind the next.
I've come to think of her now, in fact,
Or of her ghost I guess you'd have to say,
As the tear that rides and overrides
My eye, so that the edges of things go
Soft, a girl is there and not there.

*

Even in the dark
The long shadow of the stars
Drifts beneath the pines.

*

Snagged on a stalk: fresh tufts of rabbit down,
Thistle silk, a thumbnail's lot of spittle spawn.

*

Fidgeting among the goateed professors
And parlour radicals at the *Pension Russe*,
The girls whispered to themselves
About the tubercular young Reinhard,
Alone at a corner table, smoking,
Who had introduced them to immortality
By burning a cigarette paper
And as the ash plummeted upward
Exclaiming *"Die Seele fliegt!"*

*

It's the first breath of the dead
That rises from the firing squad
While the anarchist who squealed
Gets drunk and argues with God.

It's Shelley's lung in the lake
And his hand in the ashes on shore.
It's the finespun shirt he ordered
And the winding sheet he wore.

*

When the two famous novelists discovered
Each the other in the same dress –
A shot-silk "creation" of orris-dust
Laid on blanched silver, like the irony
That is the conscience of style, obscuring
To clarify, bickering to be forgiven –
One retired with her pale young admirers,
Disdain for whom creamed up in her tea,
To a folly by the buckled apple tree.
She sat and pretended to listen to herself
Being praised, picking at grizzled lichen
On the bench, like drops of blistered enamel.
The other tugged at her pearls and stayed
Near the smiles, her dress insinuated
Among the lead crystal teardrops
On the fixture above her, each one
The size, and now the colour, of a blossom
On an apple bough outside, and herself
Inside, tiny and helplessly upside down.

*

The first month of the first marriage.
The second year of the second marriage.
The third betrayal of the third marriage.
And love. Love. Always love.

*

          a deep winter yawn
                              the wind caught napping
          static on the news
                              charred ozone glaze
          dead-petal weather
                              the air's loose skin
          the albino's birthmark
                              the vinegar mother
          a bubble in the artery
                              the pebble in Demosthenes' mouth
          love asleep at the wheel
                              childhood stunned and dumped
          the philosopher's divorce
                              the psychopomp's coin
          self-pity's last tissue
                              the blister on the burn
          the emptiness added daily
                              the abstract's hive
          quarry of doubts
                              earthrise from the dark side
          the holy sleeve
                              the beatific blindness
          white root of heaven
                              the hedge around happiness

                    *

The sound of it? A silence
Understood as all the noise
Ignored or stifled, nods
Exchanged on the trading floor,
Or sex in the next room,
His hand over her mouth,
Her belt, the overcast leather,
Clenched between his teeth.
Where the needle stuck,
Its hiss and hard swallow
Halfway into the heart

Of the nocturne, two notes
Fell further apart, the space
Between them a darkness
Clotting, the moon
Having passed behind
A black key, then risen
Higher across the record's
Rutted, familiar road.

*

Suddenly, lengths of storm gauze
Drawn across the clearing.
We must not want too much
To know. Uncertainty
Condenses on the windshield,
Then runs down the cheek,
A single waxen tear.
When last night's grief
Is pulled back from,
Who will be the brighter?
Hush. Be careful. Turn
Those headlights down, low
As a curtained candle flame
Shivering in the dark dispelled.

*

First, the diagnosis: those night sweats
And thrush, the breathing that misplaces air,
The clouds gathering on a horizon of lung…
Translated as *pneumocystis*, the word from a dead
Language meant to sound like a swab
On a wound open but everywhere unseen.
Then, the options. There were options,
Left like food trays outside your door.
Protocols, support groups, diets,
A promising treatment.

                        But three months later
You began to forget the doctor's appointments,
And the next week no longer cared that you forgot.
The friends who failed to visit, even their letters
Grew hard to parse. It was not as if their "real"
Feelings lay between the lines, but that the lines
Themselves would break apart: *the fight so long*
All your work   the circumstances   remember when.
But remember was precisely what you couldn't do,
And to pay attention more than you could afford.
The books you'd read now looked back at you
With blank pages memories might fill in
With makeshift, events haphazardly recalled –
Snow swarming on the canal that Christmas
In Venice with Claudio who cried to see it,
Or globes of watery sunlight in your Chelsea flat,
White lilacs at their lips last May, no one there
For a change but just you two.
                                    And here you are
Still, propped up in the half-light, my shadow,
My likeness, your hand wandering to the arm
Of the chair, as if your fingers might trace
The chalkdust of whole years erased.
Is this, then, what it means to lose your life?
But the question is forgotten before it can be
Answered. I take your hand, and give it back
To you, and watch you then look up, giving in,
Unknowing all, whose pain has just begun.

THE WINDOW

after Pavese

Even during the war, I used to get up at noon. The weariness – a damp, musky, still warm mould of myself – stayed in bed while I made coffee. If an idea disturbed this first surface of the day – like one of those tiny whirlpools that form the closer you come to the falls – it was easily ignored. I'd stand at the window in my underwear and blow on my cup and watch them drink in the café across the square. Afternoons, I'd sit in the back of the cinema, smoking, as sad and useless as a god. Long, crumpled nylons of cigarette smoke would drift up toward the projectionist's opening, then wrap around that single beam of romance from which, in those days, everything that counted came – the orphan on the train, the machine guns and lipstick, the water ballet, the ambush in the hotel corridor. When did it start? The moment you raised your arm to wave to someone across the street? The day you didn't answer the telephone and showed up later with your hair mussed? It wasn't until the war ended and the men came home that they too realized what had happened. By then they had lived so long in the hills and cellars and hardened themselves against regret that they hadn't the energy to retrieve any delicacy of feeling. Some bought that cheap religion, love, until they had no more belief to spend. Others tried the commonplaces left out of their dreams: they made their beds in the morning and washed with plenty of soap, or stood round after round of drinks at the café', or counted on their children like the new government. Myself, I had my old habits, the letters to write to M., my diary, the dog. My train back – was it as long as a year ago now? – followed the shoreline by night. I could see little fires in the distance, and the moon laid like a compress on what beach the tide was giving up. By dawn the steam was settling on the fields. The tree-curtains parted to show a house on the crest of the hill, a lemon grove metallic against the blue sky, and then, closer, bullet-pocked, the red brick wall of a farm stable. The woman beside me had awakened by then, and asked me to help her with the window. It is easy to be good when you're not in love. You do someone a favour, and how soon you come to hate her grateful, radiant face.

KILIM

I.

The force of habit takes order to its heart,
As when a nurse, her basket filled with the dead
Child's toys, has put it by the head
Of her tomb, unwittingly on an acanthus root.

Kallimachos, they say, made his capital
Of it, when around that basket the thorny leaf
Sprang up, nature pressed down by grief
Into shapes that made the loss a parable,

His idea to change the shallow bead and reel
For an imprint of afterlife apparent to all,
Bringing down to earth an extravagance.

So skill gives way to art, or a headstone
To history – the body by now left alone,
As if bodies were the soul's ornaments.

II.

As if bodies were the soul's ornaments,
A mullah turned the Koran's carpet page.
Old Babur made a couplet instead – of Age
And Youth, his "throneless days," their violence.
The opium pearl, to ease him out of life,
Made a garden of pain. The rugs, the tent
Dissolved. A flower stall appeared. He went
On rearranging the couplet and devised,

To keep death at bay, five hundred and four
Versions. His first poem had been to a boy
From the bazaar whom for a day he had adored,

Whose glances he could still see in the dark
That lined the geometric border's void,
Reproduced in glistening egg-and-dart.

III.

Reproduction's glistening egg-and-dart,
Column or carpet, whatever cultures may rest
Upon, and couples do, like Prussian drill...
Nietzsche said the poem is a dance
In chains. Molecular life enchained by chance?
The bonds of atoms formulas distil
Are strains that resonate, the elements
Held both far together and close apart.

The rose window, its creation story speechless,
Its pattern telling all, duplicates
The cross-sectioned axial view each strand
Of genetic coil reveals. Each grain of sand
Takes an eternity to articulate
History's figure of speech for randomness.

IV.

History's figures of speech for randomness –
    Car-bomb, rape, skyjack, carcinogens,
    Dragon's teeth sown in the morning headlines,

    Blips on a monitor, all this summer's kinds
    Of long-festering terrorist violence
A final demand, its victims slumped, helpless –

How muffled they seem in my own bloodstream,
    And here in Vermont, whose coldhearted self
        Has long gone underground. The daydream
Of a hooded finch on the thistle's globe. The stealth

Of mallow colonizing clapboard. The beard
        And turban on one last old iris. Who knows
    If the image also frees what it's commandeered.
Meaning's subversive, being superimposed.

V.

Meaning, subversive because superimposed,
Signs on a dotted line of brushwood its truce,
Its terms with mountains out beyond my window's

Squaring off with cloudspray, a crest of spruce,
The green, landlocked swell and trough this state
Navigates, a chaos first unloosed

In the crown glass whose own wavering is bated
Breath upon the waters, then onto the wide
Pine floor of my study and the kilim – ornate

But frayed – that has designs on it. As if I'd
Come ashore and a moon been brought to light
The new world's passageways, its thread inside

The carpet's magic, I hear something like
So strangely silent this still desert night...

VI.

so   strangely silent   this still desert night
you kneel on me to pray   lanternlight

rows of petalled guls   to guard the borders
his knot garden opposite the women's quarters

nomad bands   a running dog   four split
leaf lobed medallions   concentric

threats   dollar signs   *God is everywhere*
a janissary comet   the mihrab's stair

and doorway   the prophet's place in his house
a sura the flame flickers on as if in doubt

the strain on paradise in its descent
hollowed out the moon jangles   the tent

pole sways   look   the heart slows
a wind that frames and fills the scene   O rose

VII.

The wind that frames and fills the scene arose
Between the mountains and the nomad camp,
Grazing the flocks, their pile of wool that combs
Had plied for spinning like stories still damp

With last night's storm of raw material,
The strands to be drawn into the spindle's plot,
Tightening for the warp, but nearly all
The weft yarn as loosely spun as thought.

Saffron, indigo, and cochineal,
The pots of dye have simmered through the night.
The loom is ready. Dawn sits by the fields
To stir. All colour is an effect of light.

The woman dreams of patterns the sky might yield,
Of love's unchanging aspect in starlight.

VIII.

And love's unchanging aspect – by starlight
          Whose cressets are blurred
     In the brazier's perfumed smoke,
A bride enters her husband's tent, her birthright
          And dowry now spread or stowed
As he sees fit, and later a child whose first
Toy is a shuttle – watches over her work.

She weaves the carpet from memory, a talent
        Her hands recollect,
    Though bound to a narrow loom
As to the tribe's own wayworn valley,
      Its tripod stakes festooned
With skeins of past and future their lives connect
When seen and heard in the fabric's page of text.

IX.

When seen and heard as one, a page of text
    And an urgent voice make up a history –
Matter, pattern, sources a poem selects.
    The carpet, too, is a complicity.
When grown at ten, the child may sit beside
    The other women and in time betray
Her mother's hand, the seed pods multiplied
    On a blank expanse, in favour of her father's way
With zigzag diagonals (he had seen
    The electric plant at Shiraz) and a few of her own
        Imaginings. By twenty she'll have learned
To read. Hafiz says love is never free
    Of choice. The rose's tongues, or its thorn alone.
        A palm-read pool, or its vacillating pattern.

X.

A palm. A red pool. The vacillating pattern
Of television lights on the bloodslick.
The diplomat still seated. The powder burn
 On his neck like a new neighbourhood picked

Out by rocket fire from the Shuf. A note,
A warning from Hezbollah, pinned to his shirt.
The day before, ten children had almost
Escaped a mortar. How much death will serve?

The assassin's mother and her mother's mother
Wove carpets. Now the time for art is past.
There is no god but God. To be a martyr
Is both thread and legend. The pistol gives her wrist
The graveside ache that, as her father's mourner,
The first stone she tossed created. And the next.

XI.

The touchstone I toss first creates but next
(Because the poem always has a shadow
Under its reliefs, unlike a carpet's
Flat entanglements, its straight and narrow
Life without illusions, turned inward
Like a dream, or like that disinterred
Necropolis Beirut's become of late –
The savagery of the abstract, form or faith –
And because that shadow is the natural world
The poem's grounded in and the figures branching
Up from it, like an oasis to the approaching
Caravan lost and found in blinding swirl
Of sand, the mirage they drink in before they turn)
Disrupts. The way things go we come to learn.

XII.

Disrupting the way things go, we come to learn,
Informs the art. Weavers incorporate
A flaw, the stitch dropped or badly turned,
To remind who kneel that only God is great,
Perfection His, His the privilege to create.
And on the block we guard or square we thread,
If thought is our element – a fiery hate,
A patient air, the earth we defend and dread –
Its flaw is the very idea that, above or ahead,
Perfection exists, the god hidden in habit.

She wakes in pain, the night cut down, her bed
A dirt floor – but there's the sun, and the stab it
Makes behind her eyes. The day's at hand.
A light signals from the mountains now, as planned.

XIII.

Some light is on the mountains now. A plan
Of the city taped to her wall, the day's targets
Marked, a red inaudible word on each…
A band of sun edges up on that paper too.
The grid of streets, the harbour's selvage, the mosques
And prismatic parks, the quadrants coloured by faction,
When brought to such a light take on a kilim's
Dispositions.
        No art can stop the killings,
Nor any point of view make an abstraction
Of the child murdered because a boundary was crossed.
The living and the dead are woven through
Us, back and forth, in and out of my speech –
The bullets' stammer, the longest threads in the carpet –
As if everything she knows I understand.

XIV.

As if everything we've known we understand,
A deal is struck. The familiar guarantee –
That for his trouble the buyer may demand
The weaver have gone blind to finish the work –
Applies. A hookah is brought. A glass of tea.
And what we've bargained for is something framed,
As night by day, an anarchy on which, alert
To lives now lost in thought, the eye is trained.

Correspondences in camouflage.
Reflected in the windowpane, we pay attention
To each in turn, the pieces of a world dislodged –
Beirut, Vermont, the surfaces that start
To yield, and depths that hold their breath, a tension
The force of habit takes as order to the heart.

XV.

The force of habit's taken order to its heart,
As if bodies were the soul's ornaments,
Reproduction's glistening egg-and-dart.
History's figures of speech for randomness –
Meaning subversive because superimposed –
Are so strangely silent this still desert night
That a wind to frame and fill the scene arose,
And love's changing aspect in starlight
We can see and hear as a single page of text,
A palm-read pool whose vacillating pattern
The touchstone I toss first creates but next
Disrupts. The way things go we come to learn.
> A light is on the mountains now, as planned,
> As if everything we've known we understand.

from
Ten Commandments
(1998)

MY EARLY HEARTS

The over-crayoned valentine ғоя мотнея.
    The furtive gym-class crush.
In my missal the polychrome Sacred Heart
    Our Saviour exposes,
The emblems of his Passion still festering,
    The knotted scourge, the sponge,
The nailhead studs all sweating blood from inside
    A little crown of thorns
Tightening around my groin as I pulled back
    The crushed-velvet curtain
And entered the confessional's dark chamber.
    Whatever lump in the throat
Aztec horror tales had once contrived to raise
    Melted in the aftermath
Of eating – myself both high priest and victim
    On his knees, head yanked back–
The live, quivering heart of thwarted romance,
    A taste one swallowed hard
First to acquire, and much later to mock.
    Hearts bid on, hearts broken.
The shape of a flame reversed in the Zippo
    Cupped close to light one last
Cigarette before walking out on a future.
    The shape two fat, rain-soaked
Paperbacks assumed on the back-porch table
    After I'd left for home,
That whole summer spent reading Tolstoy, sleeping
    With my window open
Onto an imaginary grove of birch –
    One of which I had carved
Two names on and sat under with my diary
    To watch the harvesting.
There is a black heart somewhere – the clarinet
    In K. 581,
Still aching for the pond edge, the rippling pain,
    The god's quick grasp of things.

A white one, too – that teardrop pearl on Vermeer's
    Girl at the Frick, hanging
Above her interrupted letter, mirror
    To what she's left unsaid.

At ten, on a grade-school excursion downtown
    To the science museum,
I learned my lesson once and for all – how to
    Lose myself in a heart.
In that case, a cavernous, walk-through model
    With narrow, underlit
Arterial corridors and piped-in thumps.
    As so often later,
The blindfold loosely fastened by loneliness
    Seemed to help me stumble
Past the smeary diagrams and push-button
    Explanations, helped me
Ignore the back-of-the-closet, sour-milk
    Smells and the silly jokes
Of classmates in the two-storey lung next door.
    For those others, the point
Was to end up only where they had begun,
    Back at the start of something,
Eager for the next do-it-yourself gadget.
    I stayed behind, inside,
Under the mixed blessing of not being missed.
    I could hear the old nun
Scolding some horseplay, more faintly leading them
    On to a further room,
"Where a giant pendulum will simulate
    The crisscrossed Sands of Time. ..."
What had time to do with anything *I* wanted!
    At last I had the heart
All to myself, my name echoing through it
    As I called to myself
In a stage whisper from room to blood-red room.
    And what of the smaller,
Racing heart – my own, that is – inside the heart
    Whose very emptiness
Had by now come to seem a sort of shelter?
    Was it – *me*, I mean, *my* heart –

Even back then ready to stake everything,
    To endure the trials
By fire and water, to pledge long silence,
    Accept the surprises
And sad discoveries one loses his way
    Among, walking around
And around his own heart, looking for a way
    That leads both in and out?

It happens first in one's own heart, doesn't it?
    And then in another's.
Something happens when you hear it happening.
    One day, out of the blue,
An old friend shows up and needs, so you'd thought, just
    A shoulder to cry on.
Or a new friend is stirring in the next room.
    Or the stranger in bed
Beside you gets up in the middle of the night.
    You listen for the steps.
Unfamiliar steps are coming closer, close
    Enough to reach out for.
Come over here, love. Bend down and put your head
    To my chest. Now listen.
Listen. Do you hear them? After all this time
    There are your own footsteps.
Can you hear yourself walking toward me now?

MY MAMMOGRAM

I.

In the shower, at the shaving mirror or beach,
For years I'd led... the unexamined life?
When all along and so easily within reach
(Closer even than the nonexistent wife)

Lay the trouble – naturally enough
Lurking in a useless, overlooked
Mass of fat and old newspaper stuff
About matters I regularly mistook

As a horror story for the opposite sex,
Nothing to do with what at my downtown gym
Are furtively ogled as The Guy's Pecs.

But one side is swollen, the too tender skin
Discoloured. So the doctor orders an X-
Ray, and nervously frowns at my nervous grin.

II.

Mammography's on the basement floor.
The nurse has an executioner's gentle eyes.
I start to unbutton my shirt. She shuts the door.
Fifty, male, already embarrassed by the size

Of my "breasts," I'm told to put the left one
Up on a smudged, cold, Plexiglas shelf,
Part of a robot half menacing, half glum,
Like a three-dimensional model of the Freudian self.

Angles are calculated. The computer beeps.
Saucers close on a flatness further compressed.
There's an ache near the heart neither dull nor sharp.

The room gets lethal. Casually the nurse retreats
Behind her shield. Anxiety as blithely suggests
I joke about a snapshot for my Christmas card.

III.

"No sign of cancer," the radiologist swans
In to say – with just a hint in his tone
That he's done me a personal favour – whereupon
His look darkens. "But what these pictures show...

Here, look, you'll notice the gland on the left's
Enlarged. See?" I see an aerial shot
Of Iraq, and nod. "We'll need further tests,
Of course, but I'd bet that what *you've* got

Is a liver problem. Trouble with your oestrogen
Levels. It's time, my friend, to take stock.
It happens more often than you'd think to men."

Reeling from its millionth scotch on the rocks,
In other words, my liver's sensed the end.
Why does it come as something less than a shock?

IV.

The end of life as I've known it, that is to say –
Testosterone sported like a power tie,
The matching set of drives and dreads that may
Now soon be plumped to whatever new designs

My apparently resentful, androgynous
Inner life has on me. Blind seer?
The Bearded Lady in some provincial circus?
Something that others both desire and fear.

Still, doesn't everyone *long* to be changed,
Transformed to, no matter, a higher or lower state,
To know the leathery D-Day hero's strange

Detachment, the queen bee's dreamy loll?
Oh, but the future each of us blankly awaits
Was long ago written on the genetic wall.

v.

So suppose the breasts fill out until I look
Like my own mother… ready to nurse a son,
A version of myself, the infant understood
In the end as the way my own death had come.

Or will I in a decade be back here again,,
The diagnosis this time not freakish but fatal?
The changes in one's later years all tend,
Until the last one, toward the farcical,

Each of us slowly turned into something that hurts,
Someone we no longer recognize.
If soul is the final shape I shall assume,

The shadow brightening against the fluorescent gloom,
An absence as clumsily slipped into as this shirt,
Then which of my bodies will have been the best disguise?

FOUND PARABLE

In the men's room at the office today
some wag has labelled the two stalls
    the *Erotic* and the *Political.*
The second seems suitable for the results
of my business, not for what thinking
    ordinarily accompanies it.
So I've locked myself into the first because,
though farther from the lightbulb overhead,
    it remains the more conventional
and thereby illuminating choice.
The wit on its walls is more desperate.
    As if I had written them
there myself, but only because by now
I have seen them day after day,
    I know each boast, each plea,
the runty widower's resentments,
the phone number for good head.
    Today's fresh drawing:
a woman's torso, neck to outflung knees,
with breasts like targets and at her crotch
    red felt-tip "hair" to guard
a treasure half wound, half wisecrack.
The first critic of the flesh is always
    the self-possessed sensualist.
With all that wall as his margin,
he had sniffed in smug ballpoint
    OBVIOUSLY DONE BY SOMEONE
WHO HAS NEVER SEEN THE REAL THING.
Under that, in a later hand,
    the local pinstripe aesthete
had dismissed the daydreamer's crudity
and its critic's edgy literalism.
    His block letters had squared,
not sloping shoulders: NO,
BY SOMEONE WHO JUST CAN'T DRAW.
    Were the two opinions
converging on the same moral point?

That a good drawing *is* the real thing?
    Or that the real thing
can be truly seen only through another's
    eyes? But now that I trace it through
    other jokes and members,
the bottom line leads to a higher inch
of free space on the partition –
    a perch above the loose
remarks, like the pimp's doorway
or the Zen master's cliff-face ledge.
    THERE ARE NO REAL THINGS
writes the philosopher. But he too
has been misled by everything
    the mind makes of a body.
When the torso is fleshed out
and turns over in the artist's bed,
    when the sensualist sobs over her,
when the critic buttons his pants,
when the philosopher's scorn sinks back
    from a gratified ecstasy,
then it will be clear to each
in his own way. There is nothing
    we cannot possibly not know.

MY SIDESHOW

Summers during the Eisenhower years, a carnival
Came to town. From my father's pair of bleacher seats,
The safety net under the Big Top's star attractions,
The drugged tiger, the stilted clowns, the farting scooters
All seemed as little death-defying as those routines
The high-wire trio staged with their jerky parasols.

With that singular lack of shame only a kid commands,
I'd sneak over instead to the sawdusted sideshow tent.
Every year *they* were back: the fire-breathing women,
The men who swallowed scimitars or hammered nails
Up their noses and fishhooks through their tongues,
The dwarf in his rayon jockstrap and sequined sweatband.

A buck got you into the blow-off where a taped grind
Spieled the World of Wonders while a blanket rose
On seven clear ten-gallon jars that held
Pickled fetuses – real or rubber? – their limbs
Like ampersands, each with something deliriously wrong,
Too little of this in front or too much of that behind.

Four-legged chickens, a two-headed raccoon,
The Mule-Faced Girl, the Man with Four Pupils
In His Eyes, coffined devil babies, the Penguin Boy,
The Living Skeleton, an avuncular thousand-pound
Sort who swilled cans of soda and belched at us...
What I think of the Word Made Flesh developed in this
        darkroom.

Back then I couldn't wait for hair to appear on my face
And down below, where my flashlight scrutinized at bedtime.
I'd rise and fall by chance, at the table, on buses, in class.
My voice cracked. I was shooting up and all thumbs.
Oh, the restless embarrassments of late childhood!
My first pimple – huge and lurid – had found its place.

I kept staring at one jar. The thing inside seemed to float
Up from a fishtail that was either leg or penis – or both.
(I could hear my father now, outside the tent, calling me.)
From its mouth, a pair of delicate legs emerged,
As if it had swallowed a perfect twin. I gulped. Something
Unspoken, then and since, rose like acid in my throat.

UNDER HYDRA

To disbelieve in God – or worse, in His servants –
    Of old incited mobs
With stones or stake grimly to atone for what,
    Like a bomb not lobbed
But planted in the garage of a mirror-skin
    High-rise, has from deep within
    Too suddenly exposed
The common desire to learn
    Less than had been supposed.

Bedsores, point shaving, a taste for sarongs. There are signs
    Everywhere – like the thumbprints,
Say, of thin-lipped men or sluggish women
    On an heirloom violin.
So mine is the culture of laugh track and chat room.
    Authority's foredoomed.
    Where is distance, and what
Can frighten or inspire, condemn or redeem?
    All transcendence is cut

With a canned, buttoned-down, fork-tongued cosiness.
    The stars are hooded now.
The heart's cloud chamber weeps its nuclear tears.
    My nails are bitten, and how
All-consuming my vanities, the fancied slights
    To my air-kissing appetites.
    Millennial echoes
Fill the abandoned stadium. Homeless
    Frauds crowd the two back rows.

Compel them to come in, the evangelist
    Insists. There are empty
Seats at the table for minims and ranters.
    Join the ancient family
Squabbles – whose is bigger? who deserves more?
    Prophecy's the trapdoor
    Whose fatal saving grace
Leads to listening for a voice within
    That doubles as self-praise.

His lips cut off, and flames at work on his bubbling guts,
    The wandering monk is tied
To his own refusal – a book or belief.
    The scholar, for his pride,
Is whipped, branded, and in midwinter sent out
    On the road of his doubt
    To perish of the cold.
Judge and martyr each invokes God's mercy
    On his innocent soul.

There goes the pitiful procession of mumblers,
    Slave masters and skinheads,
Witches, dealers, backwoods ayatollahs.
    And here am I, tucked in bed,
Wondering if I believe in anything more
    Than my devotions and four
    Squares. And if forced to say,
Wouldn't I deny even you, love, for a future?
    Who spoke the truth today?

PROUST IN BED

    Through the peephole he could see a boy
Playing patience on the huge crimson sofa.
   There was the carpet, the second-best
Chairs, the old chipped washstand, all his dead parents'
      Things donated months ago
     "To make an unfortunate
    Crowd happy" at the Hôtel
   Marigny, Albert's brothel,
Warehouse of desires
And useless fictions –

   For one of which he turned to Albert
And nodded, he'd have that one at cards, the soon-
   To-be footman or fancy butcher.
He'd rehearsed his questions in the corridor.
      Did you kill an animal
       Today? An ox? Did it bleed?
     Did you touch the blood? Show me
    Your hands, let me see how you...
(Judgment Day angel
Here to separate

   The Good from the Bad, to weigh the soul...
Soon enough you'll fall from grace and be nicknamed
   Pamela the Enchantress or Tool
Of the Trade. Silliness is the soul's sweetmeat.)
      One after another now,
     Doors closed on men in bed with
    The past, it was three flights to
   His room, the bedroom at last,
The goal obtained and
So a starting point

   For the next forbidden fruit – the taste
Of apricots and ripe gruyère is on the hand
   He licks – the next wide-open mouth
To slip his tongue into like a communion
     Wafer. The consolation

    Of martyrs is that the God
   For whom they suffer will see
   Their wounds, their wildernesses.
He's pulled a fresh sheet
Up over himself,

  As if waiting for his goodnight kiss
While the naked boy performs what he once did
  For himself. It's only suffering
Can make us all more than brutes, the way that boy
   Suffers the silvery thread
   To be spun inside himself,
  The snail- track left on lilac,
  Its lustrous mirror-writing,
The mysterious
Laws drawn through our lives

  Like a mother's hand through her son's hair…
But again nothing comes of it. The signal
  Must be given, the small bedside bell.
He needs his parents to engender himself,
   To worship his own body
   As he watches them adore
  Each other's. The two cages
  Are brought in like the holy
Sacrament. Slowly
The boy unveils them.

  The votive gaslights seem to flicker.
Her dying words were "What have you done to me?"
  In each cage a rat, and each rat starved
For three days, each rat furiously circling
   The pain of its own hunger.
   Side by side the two cages
  Are placed on the bed, the foot
  Of the bed, right on the sheet
Where he can see them
Down the length of his

      Body, helpless now as it waits there.
The rats' angry squealing sounds so far away.
      He looks up at his mother – touches
Himself – at her photograph on the dresser,
           His mother in her choker
              And her heavy silver frame.
        The tiny wire-mesh trapdoors
        Slide open. At once the rats
Leap at each other,
Claws, teeth, the little

    Shrieks, the flesh torn, torn desperately,
Blood spurting out everywhere, hair matted, eyes
      Blinded with the blood. Whichever stops
To eat is further torn. The half-eaten rat
          Left alive in the silver
             Cage the boy – he keeps touching
         Himself – will stick over and
         Over with a long hatpin.
Between his fingers
He holds the pearl drop.

    She leans down over the bed, her veil
Half-lifted, the scent of lilac on her glove.
      His father hates her coming to him
Like this, hates her kissing him at night like this.

TEA WITH THE LOCAL SAINT

for Jane Garmey

I'd bought a cone of solid sugar and a box
Of tea for the saint himself, a flashlight
For his son, the saint-elect, and bubblegum
For a confusion of small fry – the five-year-old
Aunt, say, and her seven-year-old nephew.
Nothing for the women, of course, the tattooed,
One-eyed, moon-faced matron, or her daughter
Whose husband had long ago run away
After killing their newborn by pouring
A bottle of cheap cologne down its throat.
This was, after all, our first meeting.

I was to be introduced by a Peace Corps pal
Whose easy, open California ways
Had brought a water system to the village
And an up-to-date word to its vocabulary.
Every other guttural spillway of Arabic
Included a carefully enunciated "awesome,"
The speaker bright-eyed with his own banter.
We sat on a pair of Kurt Cobain beach towels
And under a High-Quality Quartz Clock,
The plastic butterflies attached to whose hands
Seemed to keep time with those in my stomach.

At last, he entered the room, the saint himself,
Moulay Madani, in a white head scarf and caftan
The fading blue of a map's Moroccan coastline,
Its hem embroidered with geometric ports of call.
A rugged sixty, with a longshoreman's jaw,
A courtier's guile, and a statesman's earnest pauses,
He first explained the crescent dagger he fingered
Had been made two centuries ago by a clever Jew.
Then he squinted for my reaction. I've no taste
For bad blood, and gingerly cleared my throat to say
I was inclined to trust any saint who carried a knife.

From a copper urn, glasses of mint tea were poured,
Of a tongue-stiffening sweetness. I was allowed to wave
Away the tray of nougat– or rather, the flies on it.
Sipping, I waited for a word, a sign from the saint.
I'd wanted to lie, as if underground, and watch
Him dig up the sky, or stand at a riverbank
And have the water sweep off my presumptions,
Have him blow light into my changeling bones.
I wanted to feel the stalk rise and the blade fall.
I wanted my life's arithmetic glazed and fired.
I wanted the hush, the wingstroke, the shudder.

But sainthood, I learned soon enough, is a fate
Worse than life, nights on call for the demons
In a vomiting lamb, a dry breast, a broken radio,
And days spent parroting the timeless adages,
Spent arbitrating water rights, property lines,
Or feuds between rival herdsmen over scrub brush,
Spent blessing every bride and anyone's big-bellied
Fourth or fifth wife, praying that they deliver sons.
I thought back to the time, not ten feet from him,
I heard a homily delivered by old John XXIII,
Sounding wholly seraphic in his murmured Italian.

Ten interpreters stepped from behind the throne.
The English one at last explained the Holy Father
Had urged us all to wear seatbelts while driving.
My heart sank at its plain good sense, as hymns
Echoed and golden canopies enfolded the pope.
How like home it seemed, with my own father
A preoccupied patriarch of practicality
When what was wanted veered wildly between
The gruff headmaster and the drunken playwright.
Instead, I got the distant advertising salesman,
The suburban dad of what turned out to be my dreams....

Dreams that, decades later, back at my hotel in Fez,
A bucket of cold water was suddenly poured on.
I'd gone to the hammam, stripped, and lay on a pattern
Of sopping tiles that might have spelled God's will.
Steam shrouded the attendant methodically soaping

The knots of disappointment he'd knuckled in my back.
He paused. I drifted. [*The freezing shock.*] I looked up
At a bald, toothless gnome in swaddling clothes
On his way back to the fountain for more bad news.
Something in his bowlegged walk– perhaps the weary
Routine of it – made me think of the saint again,

Of how, when tea was done, and everyone had stood,
He reached for my head, put his hands over it,
And gently pulled me to his chest, which smelled
Of dung smoke and cinnamon and mutton grease.
I could hear his wheezy breathing now, like the prophet's
Last whispered word repeated by the faithful.
Then he prayed for what no one had time to translate –
His son interrupted the old man to tell him a group
Of snake charmers sought his blessing, and a blind thief.
The saint pushed me away, took one long look,
Then straightened my collar and nodded me toward the
    door.

CHOTT

Through the tent flap, across the air mattress, up over my
 shoulderblade,
The bandage of sunlight slips into place. On your borrowed
 Walkman

The muezzin's morning call to prayer clears its throat of
 unbelief.
Already out there pillars of sand are forming to hold up
 the sky

For minutes at a time before they buckle and collapse with
 exhaustion.
One more day on the salt flats. Air tight as a water-skin.
 Black flies

On your eyelid. Sun. Two suns, the counterfeit sun curling
 like a petal,
Separating from the true, wrenched from it to simmer on its
 reflection,

A hand's breadth between them now, the true one hauled up
 dripping.
Whose idea was a week on a dead sea anyway? A week away
 from the port,

Away from the café's chewed pits and prawnshuck, the
 feather-edged kef.
In their teaching rooms, the holy men were promising *He has
 forced*

The night and the day into your service, set forgiving mountains down
Lest the earth should move away with you. Caked mud and brine
 crust,

Like two drops of blood on a pillow, both dried to the same
 charred brick.
To reach for the newspaper risks touching you. The Jeep
 hood flutters.

Out beyond your head, slumped now over your breasts, the horizon's
Hit on the day's first mirage – lolling palms, a milky water hole,

Two Frenchmen in rockers. Is that a woman, her arm up to shade her eyes?
Or protect herself? A bronze basin over – (*Wake up, damn you! Wake. Up.*)

A mirage, the goatherd said, is always something you once had or wanted.
So by that logic, the past… no matter. It was only another promise.

Remember those first days in bed? The braided candlelight, the net of stars,
The shadow-drawn streams running underneath the body, under the loathing.

The years, the miles out and back are run through us, just sitting here.
This whole thing, it's inside a bottle, that empty fifth Hussein kept

His miniature desert in for the tourists, the dwarfed ruins he'd tweezered
Onto a dirty inch of nowhere, the how many layers of wornaway rock,

The grains of lives dry as the world's bone. Look at the sun in there,
That glistening drop of poison at the tip of the scorpion's tail.

WHAT THEY LEFT BEHIND

The room with double beds, side by side.
One was the bed of roses, still made up,
The other the bed of nails, all undone.
In the nightstand clamshell, two Marlboro butts.

On the shag, a condom with a tear in its tip
Neither of them noticed – or would even suspect
For two years more. A ballpoint embossed
By a client's firm: Malpractice Suits.

A wad of gum balled in a page of proverbs
Torn from the complimentary Bible.
His lipstick. Her aftershave.

A dream they found the next day they'd shared:
All the dogs on the island were dying
And the birds had flown up into the lonely air.

AFTER OVID

APOLLO AND HYACINTHUS

Guilt's dirty hands, memory's kitchen sink ...
        It's bad faith makes immortal love.
                Take a closer look at Hyacinth.

Dark bud-tight curls and poppy-seed stubble,
        The skin over his cheekbones pale as poison
                Slowly dripped from eye to eye,

And a crotch that whispers its single secret
        Even from behind the waiter's apron.
                He's sulking now, staring at the traffic.

Every year there's a new one at the bar
        Sprung from whatever nowhere – the country,
                The islands, the Midwest ...

The old man at the far corner table, decades ago
        Called by his critics "the sun god
                Of our poetry," sits stirring

A third coffee and an opening line,
        Something like *So often you renew*
                Yourself or *You and I resemble*

~~Nothing else~~ *Every other pair of lovers.*
        The grease stain on his left sleeve
                Winks as the lights come on.

He signals the boy and means to ask
        Under cover of settling the check
                If, with the usual understanding

And for the same pleasures, he'd return again
        Tonight, after work, there was something
                He'd wanted to show the boy, a picture

Of two sailors that if held upside down ...
        It's then he notices the gold cufflinks
                The boy is wearing, the pair the poet's

Friends had given him when his first book –
        That moist sheaf of stifled longings –
                Appeared to doting acclaim.

To have stolen from one who would give
        Anything: what better pretext
                To put an end to "an arrangement"?

The old man falls silent, gets up from his seat,
        Leaves a few coins on the table,
                And walks out through his confusions,

Homeward through the side streets, across the square,
        Up the fifty-two stone steps, up the years
                And back to his study, its iron cot.

The heaving had stopped. The last sad strokes
        Of the town clock had rung: Anger was one,
                Humiliation the other.

He sat there until dawn and wrote out the poem
        That has come to be in all the anthologies,
                The one you know, beginning

You are my sorrow and my fault. The one that goes
        In all my songs, in my mind, in my mouth
                The sighing still sounds of you.

The one that ends with the boy – the common,
        Adored, two-timing hustler – turned
                Into a flower, *the soft-fleshed lily*

But of a blotched purple that grief will come
        To scar with its initials AI, AI.
                O, the ache insists.

THE DIALOGUE OF DESIRE AND GUILT

    Even I want
  The adulterer's thrilled
Panic – the night away, the night back home.
I want to stay hard and have it both ways,
    Deaf to the heart's dull drill
        And love's cheap taunt.

Odds are someone's household gods will oblige.
    But how much of romance
        Is mere relief?
        The sound you think
  Of as longing's sigh
Finally comes clear as the moan of regret.

    The first desire
  Is to feel that one is
Desired, not just called on but called for.
I need the hindrance, too – spouse or scruple,
    A slight deformity,
        A barking dog.

The last laugh is your arrogant demand
    That the world change into
        Your wish for it.
        Go make a meal –
    Chipped beef on burnt toast points? –
Of your old quarrel with the Devouring Mom.

       The most I can
    Offer – my final bid,
Let's say – is a couple of weeks, perhaps
A month. I'm all yours. I'll eat and drink you,
    Wake and dream you, make you
       Want what I want.

The least of it is wanting. Flatterers
    Around a stuttering
       Tyrant always
       Try to guess what
    He is about to say,
Even mouth their own sudden banishment.

       Everything's called
    By a secret name, pulled
On silken threads across the eye's instant.
Let me put my hand just inside the wound,
    So warm and familiar.
       The flesh is home.

Nothing helps. The cloudy consolations,
    The zigzag alibis,
       The sodden ache
       To be alone.
    Look up at the night sky.
It's time to swallow the storm's bitter pearl.

FLIES

The agent, years ago in Argentina,
watched through a metal eyelet
in the tarpaulin as Eichmann
bought his newspaper at the kiosk.

In his report he noted the old man's
average height, bald head, large nose,
moustache, glasses, pressed tan trousers,
grey overcoat, patternless green tie.

He did not enter through the front gate
but bent under a wire marking the side
boundary of his plot and walked slowly
across the yard. A child ran up to him.

The agent couldn't see clearly. Cars went by.
The man had been leaning over,
whispering to the boy, and seemed
to be gently stroking his face,

then climbed the steps to the porch,
brushing away flies with the newspaper.
The agent felt something brush against
his face. He was about to open the door

when a stocky woman in a housecoat
opened it from inside. As he walked in,
they both absently waved to keep
the flies away from the open door.

HONEST IAGO

If ever I did dream of such a matter,
Abhor me. And remember, I know my place.
In following him, I follow but myself.
    All I want to do is help.

I'd rather have the tongue cut from my mouth
Than speak against my friend. This crack of love
Will grow stronger than it ever was before.
    There's reason to cool our raging, no?

I cannot think he means to do you any harm.
The chemotherapy seems promising.
These latest figures will show you what I mean.
    All I want to do is help.

I had not thought he was acquainted with her.
Yes, yes, this boxcar is returning to Poland.
Sure, I've already tested negative twice.
    I am bound to every act of duty.

Your sins are forgiven. This is only a phase.
I could swear it was her handkerchief I saw.
Trust me. Everything is under control.
    All I want to do is help.

AUDEN'S OED

in the old oxblood edition, the colour
    of the mother tongue, all foxed and forked,
its threadbare edges dented, once a fixture
    in the second-story Kirchstetten
room where day by day he fashioned the silence
    into objects, often sitting on
Poy-Ry, say, or *Sole-Sz*, and after his death
    sent packing from cosy Austria
to Athens, where fortune dropped it from Chester's
    trembling hands into a legacy
that exiled it next to page-curling Key West
    and finally to Connecticut,
is shelved here now, a long arm's-length from my desk.
    What he made of himself he had found
in this book, the exact weight of each soft spot
    and sore point, how each casts a shadow
understudying our hungers and our whims.
    If history is just plain dull facts,
the facts are these, these ruling nouns and upstart
    verbs, these slick adjectival toadies
and adverbial agents with their collars
    pulled up, privileged phrasal moments,
and full-scale clausal changes that qualify
    or contradict the course of a life.
This book is all we can remember and dream.
    It's how spur gears mesh and rocks are parsed
into geodes, how the blood engorges
    a glance, how the fig ripens to fall,
or what quarter-tones and quarks may signal deep
    inside a precise idea of space.
It is to this book he sat for the lessons
    the past had set him – how our Greeks died,
whom your Romans killed, how her Germans
    overreached, what his English understood,
how my Americans denied history
    was anything but an innocence
the others had simply skimmed or mispronounced.

    He knew history is a grammar,
and grammar a metaphor, and poetry
    nothing more or less than death itself –
it never lies because it never affirms.
    From the start, squinting at the propped score
with Mother in their duets at the upright
    or biting his nails while arguing
the quidditas of thuggish jacks-in-office,
    he knew what he called truth always lies
in the words and so in this dictionary,
    which like him has become a conscience
with all its roots, all its ramifications,
    meanings and examples down the years.
It was on this book he sat for the lessons
    learned five inches above a desk chair,
five inches to lean down closer to the page,
    one volume at a time, day by day,
slightly above the sense of things, but closer
    to what tomorrow so many others
will consider to have somehow been the truth.

The hard part is not so much telling the truth
    as knowing which truth to tell – or worse,
what it is you want to tell the truth, and how
    at last one learns to unlove others,
to uncast the spells, to rewind the romance
    back to its original desire
for something else altogether, its grievance,
    say, against that year's dazzling head boy
or the crippled wide-eyed horse you couldn't shoot.
    And, as innocent as the future
porno star's first milk tooth, the dictionary
    has no morality other than
definition itself. The large, functional
    Indo-European family
will do for a murky myth of origin,
    and the iron laws of shift and change
go unquestioned by the puzzled rummager.
    Our names for things tend to hold them fast
in place, give an X its features or its pitch,

      a fourth dimension of distinctness.
And what may seem vague awaits the Supplement
    just now pulling into the depot,
late as usual but looming through the steam.
    Words have their unflappable habits
of being, constellations of fixed ideas
    that still move. Sentimentality,
Snobbery, Sympathy, Sorrow – each queues up
    at the same window. No raised eyebrow
for the faked orgasm or press conference
    to issue official denials.
No sigh for the botanist's crabbed notebook.
    No praise for the florilegium.
No regret for the sinking tanker's oil slick
    glittering now off Cape Flattery.
No truck with bandbox grooming, fashion runways,
    the foot binder's stale apology,
or the dream's down payment and layaway plan.
    Everything adds up to or sinks back
into the word we know it by in this book.
    A believer in words – common prayers
or textbook theories – this wrinkled metaphor
    of the mind itself abided by
what grave and lucid laws, what keen exemptions
    these columns of small print have upheld.
He could be sitting beside one, chin in hand,
    listening to a late quartet, a gaze
on his face only the final chord will break.
    Here is that faraway something else,
here between the crowded lines of scholarship.
    Here is the first rapture and final
dread of being found out by words, terms, phrases
    for what is unknown, unfelt, unloved.
Here in the end is the language of a life.

Half my life ago, before retiring
    to new digs under Oxford's old spires,
as a part of his farewell tour of the States,
    one last look at the rooms of the house

    he'd made of our poised, mechanical largesse,
        he visited my alma mater.
    The crowd – tweedy townies and student groundlings –
        packed the hall and spilled over the lawn
    outside, where the lucky ones pressed their faces
        to windows suspense was steaming up.
    How did I find a place at the master's feet?
        My view was of the great man's ankles,
    and close enough to see his socks didn't match.
        I sat there uncomfortably but spellbound
    to his oracular mumble. And later,
        after the applause and the sherry,
    while he wambled tipsily toward his guest suite,
        I sprang as if by coincidence
    from its darkened doorway where I'd been waiting.
        But, well, waiting for *what* exactly?
    Suddenly speechless, I counted on a lie
        and told him I knew his work by heart
    and would he autograph my unread copy.
        He reached in his jacket for a pen
    and at last looked distractedly up at me.
        A pause. "Turn around and bend over,"
    he ordered in a voice vexed with impatience
        I at once mistook for genuine
    interest – almost a proposition, in fact.
        The coy young man I was then is not
    my type, but I can recognize the appeal.
        Even as I wheeled slowly around
    and put my hands on my knees, I realized
        what he wanted, what he'd asked of me.
    To write in the book, he required a desk.
        My back would do as well as any
    Tree trunk or cafeteria tabletop.
        Only years later did it make sense.
    By then I'd figured out that he'd been writing
        on me ever since that encounter,
    or that I'd unconsciously made of myself
        a desk so that he could continue –
    the common imagination's dogsbody
        and ringmaster – still to speak up,
    however halting or indirect the voice.

Today, sitting down at six to darn the day
    with a drink, I glanced across the room
to my desk, where Wystan, my month-old tabby,
    lay asleep on an open volume
of the wizard's unfailing dictionary,
    faultless creaturely Instinct atwitch
on a monument. How to sneak out past him
    for the sweating martini shaker?
My clumsy tiptoe prompts a faint annoyance –
    a single eye unlidded, a yawn,
his right paw, claws outstretched, pointing to *soodle*.
    Weren't these – the cat and book, or instinct
and idea – the two angels on his shoulder?
    Together, they'd made him suspicious
of the holy crusade, the top of the charts,
    compulsive hygiene, debt, middlemen,
seaside cottages, crooners, Gallic charm,
    public charities, the forgeries
of statecraft, the fantasies of the bedroom,
    easy assumptions, and sweeping views.
The kitten's claws have somehow caught in the page
    and puckered it so that, skewed sideways,
it resembles – or rather, for the moment
    I can make out in the lines of type –
the too often folded map his face looked like.
    Protect me, St. Wiz, protect us all
from this century by your true example.
    With what our language has come to know
about us, protect us still from both how much
    and how little we can understand
ourselves, from the unutterable blank page
    of soul, from the echoing silence
moments after the heavy book is slammed shut.

THREE DREAMS ABOUT ELIZABETH BISHOP

1.

It turned out the funeral had been delayed a year.
The casket now stood in the state capitol rotunda,
An open casket. You lay there like Lenin
Under glass, powdered, in powder blue
But crestfallen, if that's the word
For those sagging muscles that make the dead
Look grumpy. The room smelled of gardenias.
Or no, I *was* a gardenia, part of a wreath
Sent by the Radcliffe Institute and right behind
You, with a view down the line of mourners.
When Lloyd and Frank arrived, both of them
Weeping and reciting – was it "Thanatopsis"? –
A line from Frank about being the brother
To a sluggish clod was enough to wake you up.
One eye, then the other, slowly opened.
You didn't say anything, didn't have to.
You just blinked, or I did, and in another room
A group of us sat around your coffin chatting.
Once in a while you would add a comment –
That, no, hay was stacked with beaverslides,
And, yes, it was a blue, a mimeograph blue
Powder the Indians used, and stuck cedar pegs
Through their breasts in the ghost dance –
All this very slowly. Such an effort for you
To speak, as if underwater and each bubble-
Syllable had to be exhaled, leisurely
Floated up to the surface of our patience.
Still alive, days later, still laid out
In a party dress prinked with sun sparks,
Hands folded demurely across your stomach,
You lay on the back lawn, uncoffined,
Surrounded by beds of freckled foxglove
And fool-the-eye lilies that only last a day.
By then Lowell had arrived, young again
But shaggy even in his seersucker and tie.
He lay down alongside you to talk.

The pleasure of it showed in your eyes,
Widening, then fluttering with the gossip,
Though, of course, you still didn't move at all,
Just your lips, and Lowell would lean in
To listen, his ear right next to your mouth,
Then look up smiling and roll over to tell me
What you said, that since you'd passed over
You'd heard why women live longer than men –
Because they wear big diamond rings.

II.

She is sitting three pews ahead of me
At the Methodist church on Wilshire Boulevard.
I can make out one maple leaf earring
Through the upswept fog bank of her hair
– Suddenly snapped back, to stay awake.
A minister is lamenting the forgetfulness
Of the laws, and warms to his fable
About the wild oryx, "which the Egyptians
Say stands full against the Dog Star
When it rises, looks wistfully upon it,
And testifies after a sort by sneezing,
A kind of worship but a miserable knowledge."
He is wearing, now I look, the other earring,
Which catches a bluish light from the window
Behind him, palm trees bent in stained glass
Over a manger scene. The Joseph sports
A three-piece suit, fedora in hand.
Mary, in a leather jacket, is kneeling.
The gnarled lead joinder soldered behind
Gives her a bun, protruding from which
Two shafts of a halo look like chopsticks.
Intent on her task, her mouth full of pins,
She seems to be taking them out, one by one,
To fasten or fit with stars the night sky
Over the child's crib, which itself resembles
A Studebaker my parents owned after the war,
The model called an Oryx, which once took
The three of us on the flight into California.
I remember, leaving town one Sunday morning,

We passed a dwarfish, grey-haired woman
Sitting cross-legged on an iron porch chair
In red slacks and a white sleeveless blouse,
A cigarette in her hand but in a silver holder,
Watching us leave, angel or executioner,
Not caring which, pursuing her own thoughts.

III.

Dawn through a slider to the redwood deck.
Two mugs on the rail with a trace
Still of last night's vodka and bitters.
The windchimes' echo of whatever
Can't be seen. The bottlebrush
Has given up its hundred ghosts,
Each blossom a pinhead firmament,
Galaxies held in place by bristles
That sweep up the pollinated light
In their path along the season.
A scrub jay's Big Bang, the swarming
Dharma of gnats, nothing disturbs
The fixed orders but a reluctant question:
Is the world half-empty or half-full?
Through the leaves, traffic patterns
Bring the interstate to a light
Whose gears a semi seems to shift
With three knife-blade thrusts, angry
To overtake what moves on ahead.
This tree's broken under the day.
The red drips from stem to stem.
That wasn't the question. It was,
Why did we forget to talk about love?
We had all the time in the world.

What we forgot, I heard a voice
Behind me say, was everything else.
Love will leave us alone if we let it.
Besides, the world has no time for us,
The tree no questions of the flower,
One more day no help for all this night.

LATE NIGHT ODE

HORACE IV. i

It's over, love. Look at me pushing fifty now,
    Hair like grave-grass growing in both ears,
The piles and boggy prostate, the crooked penis,
    The sour taste of each day's first lie,

And that recurrent dream of years ago pulling
    A swaying bead-chain of moonlight,
Of slipping between the cool sheets of dark
    Along a body like my own, but blameless.

What good's my cut-glass conversation now,
    Now I'm so effortlessly vulgar and sad?
You get from life what you can shake from it?
    For me, it's g and t's all day and CNN.

Try the blond boychick lawyer, entry level
    At eighty grand, who pouts about the overtime,
Keeps Evian and a beeper in his locker at the gym,
    And hash in tinfoil under the office fern.

There's your hound from heaven, with buccaneer
    Curls and perfumed war-paint on his nipples.
His answering machine always has room for one more
    Slurred, embarrassed call from you-know-who.

Some nights I've laughed so hard the tears
    Won't stop. Look at me now. Why *now*?
I long ago gave up pretending to believe
    Anyone's memory will give as good as it gets.

So why these stubborn tears? And why do I dream
    Almost every night of holding you again,
Or at least of diving after you, my long-gone,
    Through the bruised unbalanced waves?

New Poems

TATTOOS

I.

Chicago, 1969

Three boots from Great Lakes stumble arm-in-arm
        Past the hookers
     And winos on South State
To a tat shack. Pissed on mai tais, what harm
        Could come from the bright slate
Of flashes on the scratcher's corridor
Wall, or the swagger of esprit de corps?

Tom, the freckled Hoosier farmboy, speaks up
        And shyly points
          To a four-inch eagle
High over the Stars and Stripes at sunup.
        A stormy upheaval
Inside – a seething felt first in the groin –
Then shoves its stubby subconscious gunpoint

Into the back of his mind. The eagle's beak
          Grips a banner
      Waiting for someone's name.
Tom mumbles that he'd like the space to read
     FELIX, for his small-framed
Latino bunkmate with the quick temper.
Felix hears his name and starts to stammer –

He's standing there beside Tom – then all three
         Nervously laugh
      Out loud, and the stencil
Is taped to Tom's chest. The needle's low-key
        Buzzing fusses until,
Oozing rills of blood like a polygraph's
Lines, there's a scene that for years won't come off.

Across the room, facedown on his own cot,
        Stripped to the waist,
    Felix wants Jesus Christ
Crucified on his shoulder blade, but not
        The heartbroken, thorn-spliced
Redeemer of punk East Harlem jailbait.
He wants light streaming from the wounds, a face

Staring right back at those who've betrayed him,
        Confident, strong,
    With a dark blue crewcut.
Twelve shading needles work around the rim
        Of a halo, bloodshot
But lustrous, whose pain is meant to prolong
His sudden resolve to fix what's been wrong.

(Six months later, a swab in Vietnam,
        He won't have time
    To notice what's been inked
At night onto the sky's open hand – palms
        Crawling with Cong. He blinks.
Bullets slam into him. He tries to climb
A wooden cross that roses now entwine.)

And last, the bookish, acned college grad
        From Tucson, Steve,
    Who's downed an extra pint
Of cut-price rye and, misquoting Conrad
        On the fate of the mind,
Asks loudly for the whole nine yards, a "sleeve,"
An arm's-length pattern of motives that weave

And eddy around shoals of muscle or bone.
        Back home he'd signed
    On for a Navy hitch
Because he'd never seen what he's since grown
        To need, an *ocean* which…
But by now he's passed out, and left its design
To the old man, whose eyes narrow, then shine.

By dawn, he's done. By dawn, the others too
        Have paid and gone.
        Propped on a tabletop
Steve's grappling with a hangover's thumbscrew.
        The bandages feel hot.
The old man's asleep in a chair. Steve yawns
And makes his way back, shielded by clip-ons.

In a week he'll unwrap himself. His wrist,
        A scalloped reef,
        Could flick an undertow
Up through the tangled swash of glaucous cyst
        And tendon kelp below
A vaccination scallop's anchored seaweed,
The swelling billow his bicep could heave

For twin dolphins to ride toward his shoulder's
        Coppery cliffs
        Until the waves, all flecked
With a glistening spume, climb the collar-
        Bone and break on his neck.
When he raises his arm, the tide's adrift
With his dreams, all his watery what-ifs,

And ebbs back down under the sheet, the past,
        The uniform.
        His skin now seems colder.
The surface of the world, he thinks, is glass,
        And the body's older,
Beckoning life shines up at us transformed
At times, moonlit, colourfast, waterborne.

II.

Figuring out the body starts with the skin,
    Its boundary, its edgy go-between,
The scarred, outspoken witness at its trials,
    The monitor of its memories,
Pleasure's flushed archivist and death's pale herald.
    But skin is general-issue, a blank

79

Identity card until it's been filled in
    Or covered up, in some way disguised
To set us apart from the beasts, whose aspects
    Are given, not chosen, and the gods
Whose repertoire of change – from shower of gold
    To carpenter's son – is limited.
We need above all to distinguish ourselves
    From one another, and ornament
Is particularity, elevating
    By the latest bit of finery,
Pain, wardrobe, extravagance, or privation
    Each above the common human herd.
The panniered skirt, dicky, ruff, and powdered wig,
    Beauty mole, Mohawk, or nipple ring,
The pencilled eyebrow above Fortuny pleats,
    The homeless addict's stolen parka,
Face lift, mukluk, ponytail, fez, dirndl, ascot,
    The starlet's lucite stiletto heels,
The billboard model with his briefs at half-mast,
    The geisha's obi, the gigolo's
Espadrilles, the war widow's décolletage…
    Any arrangement elaborates
A desire to mask that part of the world
    One's body is. Nostalgia no more
Than anarchy laces up the secondhand
    Myths we dress our well-fingered goods in.
Better still perhaps to change the body's shape
    With rings to elongate the neck, shoes
To bind the feet, lead plates wrapped to budding breasts,
    The sadhu's penis-weights and plasters,
The oiled, pumped-up torsos at Muscle Beach,
    Or corsets cinched so tightly the ribs
Protrude like a smug, rutting pouter pigeon's.
    They serve to remind us we are not
Our own bodies but anagrams of their flesh,
    And pain not a feeling but a thought.

But best of all, so say fellow travellers
    In the fetish clan, is the tattoo,
Because not merely moulded or worn awhile
    But exuded from the body's sense

Of itself, the story of its conjuring
    A means defiantly to round on
Death's insufferably endless emptiness.
    If cavemen smeared their bones with ochre,
The colour of blood and first symbol of life,
    Then peoples ever since – Egyptian
Priestesses, Mayan chieftains, woady Druids,
    Scythian nomads and Hebrew slaves,
Praetorian guards and kabuki actors,
    Hell's Angels, pilgrims, monks, and convicts –
Have marked themselves or been forcibly branded
    To signify that they are members
Of a group apart, usually above
    But often below the rest of us.
The instruments come effortlessly to hand:
    Fish bone, razor blade, bamboo sliver,
Thorn, glass, shell shard, nail, or electric needle.
    The canvas is pierced, the lines are drawn,
The colours suffuse a pattern of desire.
    The Eskimos pull a charcoaled string
Beneath the skin, and seadogs used to cover
    The art with gunpowder and set fire
To it. The explosion drove the colours in.
    Teddy boys might use matchtip sulphur
Or caked shoe polish mashed with spit. In Thailand
    The indigo was once a gecko.
In mall parlours here, India ink and tabs
    Of pigment cut with grain alcohol
Patch together tribal grids, vows, fantasies,
    Frescoes, planetary signs, pinups,
Rock idols, bar codes, all the insignia
    Of the brave face and the lonely heart.

The reasons are both remote and parallel.
    The primitive impulse was to join,
The modern to detach, oneself from the world.
    The hunter's shadowy camouflage,
The pubescent girl's fertility token,
    The warrior's lurid coat of mail,
The believer's entrée to the afterlife –
    The spiritual practicality

Of our ancestors remains a source of pride.
    Yielding to sentimentality,
Later initiates seek to dramatize
    Their jingoism, their Juliets
Or Romeos. They want to fix a moment,
    Some port of call, a hot one-night-stand,
A rush of mother-love or Satan worship.
    Superstition prompts the open eye
On the sailor's lid, the fish on his ankle.
    The biker makes a leather jacket
Of his soft beer belly and nail-bitten hands.
    The call girl's strategic butterfly
Or calla lily attracts and focuses
    Her client's interest and credit card.
But whether encoded or flaunted, there's death
    At the bottom of every tattoo.
The mark of Cain, the stigma to protect him
    From the enemy he'd created,
Must have been a skull. Once incorporated,
    Its spell is broken, its mortal grip
Loosened or laughed at or fearlessly faced down.
    A Donald Duck with drooping forelock
And swastikas for eyes, the sci-fi dragon,
    The amazon's ogress, the mazy
Yin-yang dragnets, the spiders on barbed wire webs,
    The talismanic fangs and jesters,
Ankhs and salamanders, scorpions and dice,
    All are meant to soothe the savage breast
Or back beneath whose dyed flesh there beats something
    That will stop. Better never to be
Naked again than not disguise what time will
    Press like a flower in its notebook,
Will score and splotch, rot, erode, and finish off.
    Ugly heads are raised against our end.
If others are unnerved, why not death itself?
    If unique, then why not immortal?
Protected by totem animals that perch
    Or coil in strategic locations –
A lizard just behind the ear, a tiger's
    Fangs seeming to rip open the chest,
An eagle spreading its wings across the back –
    The body at once both draws death down

And threatens its dominion. The pain endured
    To thwart the greater pain is nothing
Next to the notion of nothingness.
    Is that what I see in the mirror?
The vacancy of everything behind me,
    The eye that now takes so little in,
The unmarked skin, the soul without privileges ...
    Everything's exposed to no purpose.
The tears leave no trace of their grief on my face.
    My gifts are never packaged, never
Teasingly postponed by the need to undo
    The puzzled perfections of surface.
All over I am open to whatever
    You may make of me, and death soon will,
Its unmarked grave the shape of things to come,
    The page there was no time to write on.

III.

    New Zealand, 1890

Because he was the chieftain's eldest son
    And so himself
    Destined one day to rule,
The great meetinghouse was garishly strung
    With smoked heads and armfuls
Of flax, the kiwi cloak, the lithograph
    Of Queen Victoria, seated and stiff,

Oil lamps, the greenstone clubs and treasure box
    Carved with demons
    In polished attitudes
That held the tribal feathers and ear drops.
    Kettles of fern root, stewed
Dog, mulberry, crayfish and yam were hung
To wait over the fire's spluttering tongues.

The boy was led in. It was the last day
                Of his ordeal.
    The tenderest sections –
Under his eyes, inside his ears – remained
            To be cut, the maze run
To its dizzying ends, a waterwheel
Lapping his flesh the better to reveal

Its false-face of unchanging hostility.
              A feeding tube
    Was put between his lips.
His arms and legs were held down forcibly.
          Resin and lichen, mixed
With pigeon fat and burnt to soot, was scooped
Into mussel shells. The women withdrew.

By then the boy had slowly turned his head,
              Whether to watch
    Them leave or keep his eye
On the stooped, greyhaired cutter who was led
           In amidst the men's cries
Of ceremonial anger at each
Of the night's cloudless hours on its path

Through the boy's life. The cutter knelt beside
            The boy and stroked
    The new scars, the smooth skin.
From his set of whalebone chisels he tied
          The shortest one with thin
Leather thongs to a wooden handle soaked
In rancid oil. Only his trembling throat

Betrayed the boy. The cutter smiled and took
              A small mallet,
    Laid the chisel along
The cheekbone, and tapped so a sharpness struck
           The skin like a bygone
Memory of other pain, other threats.
Someone dabbed at the blood. Someone else led

A growling chant about their ancestors.
                Beside the eye's
     Spongy marshland a frond
Sprouted, a jagged gash to which occurs
          A symmetrical form,
While another chisel pecks in the dye,
A blue the deep furrow intensifies.

The boy's eyes are fluttering now, rolling
              Back in his head.
     The cutter stops only
To loop the blade into a spiralling,
         Puckered, thick filigree
Whose swollen tracery, it seems, has led
 The boy beyond the living and the dead.

He can feel the nine Nothings drift past him
              In the dark: Night,
     The Great Night, the Choking
Night, the All-Brightening Night and the Dim,
         The Long Night, the Floating
Night, the Empty Night, and with the first light
A surging called the War Canoe of Night –

Which carries Sky Father and Earth Mother,
            Their six sons borne
     Inside the airless black
The two make, clasped only to each other.
         Turning onto his back,
The eldest son struggles with all his force,
Shoulder to sky, straining until it's torn

Violently away from the bleeding earth.
             He sets four beams,
     Named for the winds, to keep
His parents apart. They're weeping, the curve
         Of loneliness complete
Between them now. The old father's tears gleam
Like stars, then fall as aimlessly as dreams

To earth, which waits for them all to return.
              Hers is the care
        Of the dead, and his tears
Seep into her folds like a dye that burns.
        One last huge drop appears
Hanging over the boy's head. Wincing, scared,
He's put his hand up into the cold air.

GLANUM

at the ruins of a provincial Roman town

So this is the city of love.
I lean on a rail above
Its ruined streets and square
Still wondering how to care
For a studiously unbuilt site
Now walled and roofed with light.
A glider's wing overhead
Eclipses the Nike treads
On a path once freshly swept
Where trader and merchant kept
A guarded company.
As far as the eye can see
The pampered gods had blessed
The temples, the gates, the harvest,
The baths and sacred spring,
Sistrum, beacon, bowstring.
Each man remembered his visit
To the capital's exquisite
Libraries or whores.
The women gossiped more
About the one-legged crow
Found in a portico
Of the forum, an omen
That sluggish priests again
Insisted required prayer.
A son's corpse elsewhere
Was wrapped in a linen shroud.
A distant thundercloud
Mimicked a slumping pine
That tendrils of grape entwined.
Someone kicked a dog.
The orator's catalogue
Prompted worried nods
Over issues soon forgot.
A cock turned on a spit.
A slave felt homesick.

The underclass of scribes
Was saved from envy by pride.
The always invisible legion
Fought what it would become.

*

We call it ordinary
Life – banal, wary,
Able to withdraw
From chaos or the law,
Intent on the body's tides
And the mysteries disguised
At the bedside or the hearth,
Where all things come apart.
There must have been a point –
While stone to stone was joined,
All expectation and sweat,
The cautious haste of the outset –
When the city being built,
In its chalky thrust and tilt,
Resembled just for a day
What's now a labelled display,
These relics of the past,
A history recast
As remarkable rubble,
Broken column, muddled
Inscription back when
Only half up, half done.
Now only the ruins are left,
A wall some bricks suggest,
A doorway into nothing,
Last year's scaffolding.
By design the eye is drawn
To something undergone.
A single carving remains
The plunder never claimed,
And no memories of guilt
Can wear upon or thrill
This scarred relief of a man
And woman whom love will strand,

Their faces worn away,
Their heartache underplayed,
Just turning as if to find
Something to put behind
Them, an emptiness
Of uncarved rock, an excess
Of sharp corrosive doubt.

*

Now everything's left out
To rain and wind and star,
Nature's repertoire
Of indifference or gloom.
This French blue afternoon,
For instance, how easily
The light falls on debris,
How calmly the valley awaits
Whatever tonight frustrates,
How quickly the small creatures
Scurry from the sunlight's slur,
How closely it all comes to seem
Like details on the table between
Us at dinner yesterday,
Our slab of sandstone laid
With emblems for a meal.
Knife and fork. A deal.
Thistle-prick. Hollow bone.
The olive's flesh and stone.

J. D. McCLATCHY is the author of five collections of poetry: *Scenes from Another Life* (1981), *Stars Principal* (1986), *The Rest of the Way* (1990), *Ten Commandments* (1998) and *Hazmat* (2002). His literary essays have been collected in *White Paper* (1989) and *Twenty Questions* (1998). He has written several opera libretti, and edited many other books. A Chancellor of the Academy of American Poets and a member of the American Academy of Arts and Letters, he teaches at Yale University, and since 1991 has been editor of *The Yale Review*.

Also available in the
ARC PUBLICATIONS
International Poets series

LOUIS ARMAND (Australia)
Inexorable Weather

MICHAEL AUGUSTIN (Germany)
A Certain Koslowski
(prose humour)
TRANSLATED FROM THE GERMAN BY MARGITT LEHBERT
ILLUSTRATED BY HARTMUT EING

ROSE AUSLÄNDER (Germany)
Mother Tongue
TRANSLATED FROM THE GERMAN
BY JEAN BOASE-BEIER AND ANTHONY VIVIS

DON COLES (Canada)
Someone has Stayed in Stockholm

SARAH DAY (Australia)
New & Selected Poems

GAIL DENDY (South Africa)
Painting the Bamboo Tree

KATHERINE GALLAGHER (Australia)
Tigers on the Silk Road

ROBERT GRAY (Australia)
Lineations

MICHAEL S. HARPER (U.S.A)
Selected Poems

DENNIS HASKELL (Australia)
Samuel Johnson in Marrickville

DINAH HAWKEN (New Zealand)
Small Stories of Devotion

ANDREW JOHNSTON (New Zealand)
The Open Window

JOHN KINSELLA (Australia)
The Undertow
The Silo:
A PASTORAL SYMPHONY

EVA LIPSKA (Poland)
Pet Shops & Other Poems
PARALLEL-TEXT EDITION POLISH / ENGLISH, TRANSLATED FROM THE
POLISH BY BARBARA BOGOCZEK AND TONY HOWARD

CONLETH O'CONNOR (Ireland)
Night without Stars, Days Without Sun

MICHAEL O'LOUGHLIN (Ireland)
Another Nation

MARY JO SALTER (U.S.A.)
A Kiss in Space

TOMAZ SALAMUN (Slovenia)
Homage to Hat and
Uncle Guido and Eliot
SELECTED POEMS
EDITED BY CHARLES SIMIC, INTRODUCTION ROBERT HASS,
TRANSLATED FROM THE SLOVENE BY
CHARLES SIMIC, ANSELM HOLLO ETC.

C.K. STEAD (New Zealand)
Straw into Gold
The Right Thing

ANDREW TAYLOR (Australia)
The Stone Threshold

JOHN TRANTER (Australia)
The Floor of Heaven